ANIMAL PREDATORS

Wolves

SANDRA MARKLE

LERNER PUBLICATIONS / MINNEAPOLIS

THE ANIMAL WORLD IS FULL OF
PREDATORS.

Predators are the hunters who find, catch, and eat other animals—their prey—in order to survive. Every environment has its chain of hunters. The smaller, slower, less able predators become prey for the bigger, faster, more cunning hunters. And everywhere, there are just a few kinds of predators at the top of the food chain. *In the far northern forests of the world and in the windswept Arctic, one of these is the wolf.*

Late in the afternoon, these gray wolves set off across the snow-covered high meadow, on a long hunt searching for prey. They lope along single file, following the alpha male wolf, the leader and one of the group's strongest hunters.

The alpha male stands 31 inches (79 centimeters) tall at the shoulder. His long legs make the trail-breaking job easier because he's tall enough to walk through most drifts. The wolves behind him, following in his footprints, don't have to use as much energy on the snow-covered trail. The youngest, smallest wolves at the end of the line trot easily over the packed-down snow.

Finally, the wolves reach the forest. Sniffing the snow-covered ground, several of the wolves whimper excitedly. They've detected the familiar scent of moose. For a wolf, the world is shaped as much by what it smells as by what it sees. A wolf's long nose is lined with cells that pick up scents. A wolf's sense of smell is so keen it can detect prey as far as 1 mile (more than 1 kilometer) away. Wolves can even detect a faint hint of a prey animal that walked over the ground several days earlier.

The wolves move in, following their noses toward the source of the scent. As they get closer, they hear the sounds of the moose. A wolf's ears are sound scoops. The wolves turn their ears to detect where the sound is loudest.

By the time the wolves are close enough to see their prey, the moose know that the wolves are coming. A moose's big ears are sound scoops too, and large eyes on the sides of its head let the moose see nearly all the way around itself. At the sight of the approaching wolf pack, the pair of moose split up. Running, each moose takes its own escape route through the forest.

Wolves are part of a group, a pack, that uses teamwork to catch prey. The wolves focus on one of the escaping moose and chase after it.

Trying to escape the hunters, the moose heads deeper into the forest. The moose's long legs let it run easily through the snow.

It takes more energy for the wolves to plow through deep drifts. So the wolves take turns charging the moose to keep it running. Meanwhile, the rest of the pack follows, with each wolf taking the easiest route it can find. Younger and less strong members of the pack come along behind, running in a path that has already been broken for them.

A moose can kick hard enough to break a wolf's jaw, so the wolves keep their distance until the moose, nearly exhausted, stops and turns to face its attackers. Then the alpha female leaps, raking the moose's side with her teeth before darting safely out of kicking range.

The pack joins the attack, leaping and biting wherever they can. The moose breaks free, but it manages to run only a short distance before two members of the pack catch up. They attack together, biting the moose's legs.

The alpha male attacks the moose, biting and ripping the moose's flesh. A wolf's main weapons are its powerful jaws, armed with forty-two sharp teeth. Its four sharp canines are each almost 2 inches (5 cm) long. The pack quickly joins in the attack. Within minutes, the moose is dead.

As quickly as the battle is finished, the pack's team spirit is forgotten. The wolves fight among themselves as they compete for a share of the kill.

With nips and snarls, the alpha male and female quickly establish dominance—that they are the leaders. They tear into the moose, claiming their share. Then the rest of the pack joins in the feast.

Wolves eat mainly meat because their stomachs work best breaking down flesh and fat. An adult wolf needs about 5 pounds (about 2 kilograms) of meat every day to stay strong and healthy, but it isn't likely to catch big prey every day. So when the pack makes a big kill, each wolf gulps down as much as its stomach can hold—as much as 20 pounds (9 kg) of meat.

With bulging, full stomachs, the wolves curl up in the snow, wrapping their long, bushy tails over their feet and noses. Sleeping is a good way to conserve energy for the next hunt.

Scavengers, such as ravens and foxes, will feed off the remains of the kill too. They and the gray wolves will keep returning to the kill until the bones are picked clean. The wolves' powerful jaws even let them crack open the long bones of the moose to feed on the marrow, the fatty material inside the bones. If prey animals are plentiful, the wolves may cache, or bury, large chunks of meat. Their sensitive noses will let them find these leftovers to feed on later when prey is hard to find.

All winter long, the search for food goes on. When the pack can't find big prey to share, the individual members must hunt for themselves. Sometimes a meal may be no more than an arctic hare.

If the pack is lucky, the wolves will bring down another large animal, such as a deer or elk. All winter, the big grazing animals are on the move, searching for food. The wolves stay on the move too, searching for these prey animals.

To give the pack the best possible chance for success, the wolves stay in their own hunting territory. Working in an area it knows well, the pack avoids competing with other wolves for the limited supply of big prey. To prevent neighboring packs from meeting each other, the pack members announce where they are by howling. They also scent mark their territory by urinating along the borders.

Finally, spring arrives. The days are longer, and the snow covering the high meadows melts. Soon the only remaining drifts are tucked like white shadows under rock ledges and the spreading branches of giant pines. While the mother deer chomps the tender new grass, her fawn hides among the shadows on the forest floor.

The young deer's spotted coat makes it hard to see. But the wolves can detect the fawn's scent and track it down. Deer, elk, and moose all give birth in the spring. Hunting their young is easy, and wolf pack members often go out alone.

Between hunts, the pack reunites at a meeting site near a den, which is a cave or a tunnel dug into the earth. Safe inside this den, the alpha female gives birth to a trio of pups—the pack's only offspring.

At first, the tiny pups are completely helpless. Their eyes are sealed shut. They don't have any teeth. They can't even produce enough body heat to warm themselves. For the first three weeks of the pups' lives, the female supplies all their needs. She curls around the pups to keep them warm and lets them suckle her rich milk. After the pups eat, she licks their tummies to get them to pass wastes. Then she licks up the wastes to keep the den free of any telltale scents that could attract a hungry mountain lion or grizzly bear. When wolves are small, these future predators are in danger of becoming prey themselves.

By the time the pups are three weeks old, they've grown enough to leave the den. Their mother carries them out in her jaws, one by one, to meet the other members of the pack.

From then on, the whole pack helps raise the pups. Because the alpha female is one of the strongest members of the pack, she returns to hunting while another wolf stays behind to pup-sit.

In addition to their mother's milk, the pups are now fed meat that is partly digested. When the pack returns from a hunt, each pup rushes up to one of the adults, whimpering and licking the adult's mouth. This triggers the adult to throw up some of the food in its stomach for the pup to eat.

Before long, the tired adults settle down to sleep, but the pups are eager to explore the world. Spotting a frog at the edge of the stream, one pup stalks it. Just as the pup pounces, the frog leaps into the water and escapes. This play is the pup's first lesson in learning how to hunt.

Next, the pups attack a piece of deerskin left from a recent kill. Growling as though making their own kill, they bite and tug until the skin rips apart.

By the time they are four months old, the gray wolf pups have grown big enough to become hunters in training. Their sense of smell has sharpened, and their adult teeth are coming in. Their feet have developed tough toe pads, and their legs are long enough for them to run through streams and tall grass.

In the far north, young arctic wolves are learning to hunt too. Prey is often scarce in this rugged land. When they get the chance, arctic wolves hunt big animals such as musk oxen. Then they will have enough food to last for several days. On the other hand, a musk ox isn't easy prey. So when an arctic wolf pack goes after a herd of musk oxen, every member of the pack is needed—even the youngest hunters.

There aren't any trees or shrubs to provide cover this far north, so the wolves circle in the open, staying downwind. When a big adult ox grunts an alarm, the oxen herd begins to form a protective circle around its three calves. The alpha female wolf charges to break up the herd.

The wolf pack singles out one calf and closes in. The alpha male wolf attacks first. The best plan would be for the young wolves to bite the calf's legs to slow it down. Instead, the inexperienced youngsters mimic their father and bite the calf's neck. Still, the pack's shared effort is enough to overpower the calf. Within minutes, the calf is dead. This is the first of many kills the young wolves will help their pack make.

Each year, as new pups are born and grow up, the wolf packs of the world have a better chance of surviving. That's because, once again, these hunting families have become one generation stronger.

Looking Back

- Check out the running wolf on page 12. A wolf's chest is very narrow, so its front legs are close together. In fact, as a wolf runs, its front feet strike the ground, one after the other, in nearly the same spot.

- Look at the wolf's teeth on page 14. See how the sharp upper and lower teeth fit together? The teeth can snip right through the skin of the wolf's prey.

- Look closely at the wolves' fur coats on page 21. The long outer guard hairs act like a raincoat to shed water. The wooly undercoat is like long underwear, trapping body heat. A wolf also has bristly hairs around its toes to help protect its feet from the cold.

- Take another look at the wolf on page 25. A wolf's two forward facing eyes help it judge how far it has to leap to bite its prey.

- Read again about the features the moose (pages 8 through 14) and the musk oxen (pages 34 through 37) have to protect themselves from wolves. What defenses do these prey animals have in common?

Glossary

ALPHA WOLVES: the strongest, dominant members of the pack. The pack is led by an alpha male and female. They are usually the only pair to mate and produce offspring.

CACHE: chunks of meat buried by wolves when food is plentiful and dug up when food is scarce

DEN: a hidden home, such as a burrow or cave, used by the alpha female wolf when her pups are born

HERD: a group of the same kind of animal, which feeds and travels together

HOWL: a long, wavering sound produced by a wolf to help the pack reunite, to signal territorial rights, or just because they want to

MARROW: the soft fatty material that fills the central cavity of bones

MUSK OX: a large wild ox found in the Arctic areas of Canada and Greenland. Its name comes from the strong odor produced by the males during the breeding season.

PACK: a group of wolves that lives and hunts together

PREDATOR: an animal that is a hunter

PREY: an animal that a predator catches to eat

TERRITORY: the area within which a wolf pack usually hunts

TOOTH: a hard, sharp structure in the wolf's mouth for biting and chewing. An adult wolf has forty-two teeth.

Further Information

Books

Brandenburg, Jim, and Joann Bren Guernsey. *To the Top of the World: Adventures with Arctic Wolves.* New York: Walker, 1995. Learn about a wildlife photographer's experiences living with an arctic wolf pack.

Johnson, Sylvia A., and Alice Aamodt. *Wolf Pack: Tracking Wolves in the Wild.* Minneapolis: Lerner Publications Company, 1985. Learn about wolf packs and the ways they are studied by scientists.

Markle, Sandra. *Growing Up Wild: Wolves.* New York: Atheneum, 2001. Text and photos describe the development of gray wolves during the several seasons it takes them to mature.

Simon, Seymour. *Wolves.* New York: HarperTrophy, 1995. This book describes life within the wolf pack.

Swinburne, Stephen R. *Once a Wolf: How Wildlife Biologists Fought to Bring Back the Gray Wolf.* Boston: Houghton Mifflin, 1995. This book explores the efforts to return wolves to Yellowstone National Park.

Videos

Wolves—A Legend Returns to Yellowstone (National Geographic, 1999). This film follows one of the wolf packs introduced into Yellowstone Park.

Wolves at Our Door (Discovery Home Video, 2000). This film follows a pack of wolves raised by a human couple, showing the wolves' development and behavior.

Index

For my good friend Andrea Platt, with love

The author would like to thank Dr. Eric Gese, Research Wildlife Biologist and Assistant Professor, National Wildlife Research Center, Department of Fisheries and Wildlife, Utah State University-Logan for sharing his expertise and enthusiasm. As always, a special thanks to Skip Jeffery, for his help and support.

Photo Acknowledgments

The photographs in this book are reproduced with the permission of: © Erwin & Peggy Bauer, pp. 1, 4, 28, 34; © Jim Brandenburg/ Minden Pictures, pp. 3, 16, 18, 21, 35, 36; © Daniel J. Cox/natural exposures.com, pp. 6, 12, 24; © Rolf Peterson, pp. 7, 8, 11, 13, 17; © Erwin & Peggy Bauer/Bruce Coleman, Inc., pp. 9, 25, 33; © Gordon & Cathy Illg/Animals Animals, p. 14; © Tim Fitzharris/Minden Pictures, p. 15; © Tom Brakefield/Bruce Coleman, Inc., p. 20; © Jessica A. Ehlers/Bruce Coleman, Inc., p. 23; © Rich Kirchner, pp. 27, 29; © Art Wolfe, p. 30; © Tom and Pat Leeson, pp. 31, 32.
Cover: © John Shaw/Bruce Coleman, Inc.
Back cover: © Jessica A. Ehlers/Bruce Coleman, Inc.

Lerner Publications Company
A division of Lerner Publishing Group, Inc.
241 First Avenue North
Minneapolis, MN 55401 USA

For reading levels and more information, look up this title at www.lernerbooks.com.

Library of Congress Cataloging-in-Publication Data

Markle, Sandra.
  Wolves / by Sandra Markle.
    p.   cm.—(Animal predators)
  Summary: An introduction to the lives of wolves which focuses on how they hunt and how they raise their cubs.
  Includes index.
  ISBN-13: 978−1−57505−732−3 (lib. bdg. : alk. paper)
  ISBN-10: 1−57505−732−8 (lib. bdg. : alk. paper)
  ISBN-13: 978−1−57505−748−4 (pbk. : alk. paper)
  ISBN-10: 1−57505−748−4 (pbk. : alk. paper)
  1. Wolves—Juvenile literature. [1. Wolves.] I. Title.
QL737.C22M364 2004
599.773—dc21   2003011197

Manufactured in the United States of America
6-44055-3583-4/28/2017